MRCP Part II
Examination Handbook

Author & Editor:

Sanjay Sharma BSc (Hons) MRCP (UK) MD
Senior Specialist Registrar Cardiology
St Georges Hospital, London, England
Senior Lecturer for Medipass
Medical Director for medibyte.com

Contributors:
Sam Firoozi BSc (Hons) MRCP (UK)
Research Fellow Cardiology
St Georges Hospital, London, England

Rashmi Kaushal BSc (Hons) MRCP (UK)
Research Fellow Endocrinology
St Georges Hospital, London, England

Sandpiper Publishing
Blackwater Lodge Shop Lane
East Mersea Colchester
Essex CO5 8TR

Tel: +44 (0) 1206 382271
Fax: +44 (0) 1206 382271
E Mail: salmonese@btinternet.com

ISBN 0-9538606-0-4

Introduction

The MRCP examination in general medicine is the most popular post-graduate examination in the world! It is geared to teach more than it actually tests and the knowledge acquired during preparation for the exam remains invaluable for an indefinite period. Passing the examination is a major stepping stone for a junior doctor wishing to embark on a career in hospital medicine. The standards are high and competition stiff, therefore thorough preparation is essential to maximise the chances of success. This is best performed by attempting as many case histories, data interpretation and slide questions as possible and reading around any deficiencies in knowledge highlighted by them. This small book provides a selection of 50 questions which should prove useful for the MRCP examination.

Abbreviations

ACTH	adrenocorticotrophic hormone	DHEAS	dehydroepiandrost-enedione sulphate
ADH	anti-diruretic hormone	DVT	deep vein thrombosis
Alk Phos	alkaline phosphate	ESR	erythrocyte sedimentation rate
AST	aspartate transaminase		
ARVC	arrhythmogenic right ventricular cardiomyopathy	ECG	electrocardiogram
		ECHO	echocardiogram
		EEG	electroencephalogram
AV	aortic valve	FBC	full blood count
ANF	anti-nucleur factor	FSH	follicle stimulating hormone
APTT	activated partial prothrombin time	FEV	forced expiritory volume
AXR	abdominal X-ray	FVC	forced vital capacity
AF	atrial fibrillation	GGT	gamma-glutamyl transferase
ARF	acute renal failure		
APCKD	acute polycystic kidney disease	Hb	haemoglobin
		Hep B	hepatitis B
ALT	alanine transaminase	HCM	hypertrophic cardiomyopathy
ABG	arterial blood gas		
ANCA	anti-neutrophil cytoplasmic antibodies	HIV	human immunodeficiency virus
CSF	cerebrospinal fluid	JVP	jugular venous pressure
CT	computed tomography	KCO	corrected carbon monoxide transfer factor
CMV	cytomegalovirus		
COAD	chronic obstructive airways disease	LFT	liver function tests
		LH	leutinizing hormone
CXR	chest X-ray	LBBB	left bundle branch block
CRP	C-reactive protein	LFT	liver function tests

LV	left ventricle
MSU	mid stream urine
MCHC	mean cell haemoglobin concentration
MCV	mean cell volume
PA	pulmonary artery
PT	prothrombin time
PTH	parathyroid hormone
PCWP	pulmonary capillary wedge pressure
RBBB	Right bundle branch block
RV	right ventricle/residual volume
SLE	systemic lupus erythematosis
SIADH	syndrome of inappropriate anti-diruretic hormone
TCLO	total lung carbon monoxide transfer factor
TFT	thyroid function tests
TLC	total lung capacity
TB	tuberculosis
U&E	urea and electrolytes
VT	ventricular tachycardia
VQ	ventilation/perfusion scan
WCC	white cell count
ZN Stain	Ziehl-Neelsen stain

A 45 year old social worker presents with a 12 month history of depression and a 4 month history of muscle weakness affecting his thighs and his arms. He admits that stress may have resulted in him drinking slightly more alcohol than usual.

On examination, he is obese (Figure A) with a BP of 170/110 mm.Hg and has evidence of bruising on his left shin.

Investigations:

Normal U&E, LFT's and γGT.

1. What is the most likely diagnosis?
2. What single investigation will assist you with the exclusion of possible differentials?

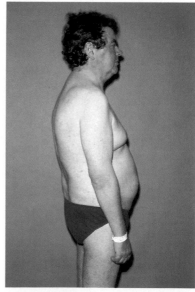

Figure A

A 27 year old woman presents with a 6 week history of generalised headaches and malaise.

Investigations:

CSF Findings are as follows:

CSF	210mm H_2O	
Cells	White Cells	50/mm^3 (85% lymphocytes)
	Red Cells	4/mm^3
	Protein	1.3 g/l
	Glucose	2.9 mmol/l (blood glucose 5 mmol/l)

1. List two possible diagnoses.
2. List one test for each which could be performed on the CSF to confirm the diagnosis.

Question 3

A 63 year old smoker presents with a 3 month history of weight loss of 13 kg.

On examination he appears sun tanned and there is evidence of reduced power in proximal distribution affecting his legs.

Investigations:

Sodium	143 mmol/l
Potassium	3.1 mmol/l
Urea	4.2 mmol/l
Creatinine	102 mmol/l
9.00am Cortisol	860 nmol (150-650 nmol)
9.00am ACTH	728 ng (<50 ng/l)
CT Pituitary: No focal abnormality seen	
CT Thorax: No focal abnormality seen	
Whole body venous sampling for ACTH ng/l:	

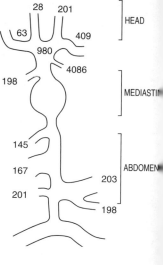

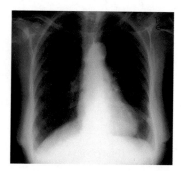

1. What is the most likely diagnosis?

Question 4

A 33 year old lady presents with a 2 week history of anterior neck pain radiating to her right ear and mandible. She also describes a general feeling of malaise and had a low grade fever preceding the neck pain by a few weeks. She has lost 3.18 kg and claims that she is feeling very nervous.
On examination, she has a pulse of 100 beats per minute and complains of discomfort when her neck is palpated.

Investigations:

Hb	11.1 g/dl
WCC	9 x 10⁹/l
Platelets	254 x 10⁹/l
ESR	30 mm/h
Free T4	28 pmol/l (11-23)
TSH	0.11 mu/l (0.5-4.0)

1. What is the diagnosis?
2. What investigation will confirm this?
3. What is the treatment?

Question 5

A 60 year old man was referred to the dermatology clinic with chronic leg ulcers and immobility. On examination, he was obese with evidence of gynecomastia. He attributed his weight problem to the fact that he was lonely and that he had no family or friends. He had just one heterosexual relationship in his twenties which ended due to sexual problems.

Investigations:

Random Glucose	12.2 mmol/l
Testosterone	3.2 (9-24 nmol/l)
LH	18.4 (1-9 iu/l)
FSH	21.3 (1-10 iu/l)
Prolactin	286 mu/l

1. Comment on the results
2. What is the likely diagnosis?

Question 6

A 25 year old asian overseas student presents with a 3 year history of aching hips and legs and fatigue. Her symptoms improve when she returns to India for the summer holiday but recur on her return.

She has few friends and her college principal suspects that she may be depressed.

Investigations:

Hb	12.1 g/dl
WCC	$7.2 \times 10^9/l$
Platelets	$268 \times 10^9/l$
Corrected calcium	2.10 mmol/l
Phosphate	0.98 mmol/l
Alk phos	450 iu/l

1. List 2 investigations that would assist with the diagnosis.
2. What is the likely diagnosis?

Question 7

A 48 year old lady presents with an 8 month history of thirst and polydipsia.

She has developed nocturia at a frequency of two times a night and headaches. She also complains of weakness affecting her legs.

She is not on any regular medication.

On examination her blood pressure was 170/105 mm.Hg. There were no stigmata of cardiac or liver disease.

Investigations:

Random blood glucose	6.8 mmol/l
Sodium	149 mmol/l
Potassium	3.2 mmol/l
Urea	4.1 mmol/l
Creatinine	68 μmol/l

1. What is the likely diagnosis?
2. List 2 investigations that would help to confirm this.

Question 8

A 12 year old boy presents with a 1 year history of pain affecting his hands and feet. He experienced 2 episodes in the last 3 months when the pain was so severe that he was taken to casualty. He describes a burning pain and when seen in A&E he is found to have a low grade fever of 37.7°C. There are a number of telangiectasia located at the umbilicus, penis, scrotum, buttocks and thighs.

Investigations:

Sodium	142 mmol/l
Potassium	5.6 mmol/l
Urea	22.6 mmol/l
Creatinine	342 μmol/l

He is referred to a paediatrician who examines his eyes and observes evidence of corneal atrophy. Urinalysis reveals proteinuria +1 and bifringent lipid molecules.

1. What is the diagnosis?
2. What further investigations will assist you in making the diagnosis?
3. List 3 steps in the management of this condition.

Question 9

A 26 year old overweight lady who is 7 days post partum complains of right upper quadrant pain, malaise and flu like symptoms. She developed a high blood pressure of 140/98 mm.Hg towards the end of her pregnancy but did not have proteinuria. She is seen by the surgical registrar who diagnoses biliary colic. He requests a number of blood tests and starts her on antibiotics.

Investigations:

Hb	11.1 g/dl
WCC	7.8 x 10⁹/l
Platelets	41 x 10⁹/l
Blood film	(Figure A)
Sodium	143 mmol/l
Potassium	5.8 mmol/l
Urea	21.2 mmol/l
Creatinine	585 μmol/l
Bilirubin	109 μmol/l
AST	120 iu/l
ALT	54 iu/l
Alk Phos	100 iu/l

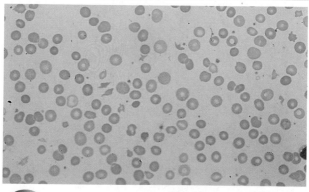

Figure A

She becomes more unwell over the next 24 hours and develops generalised seizures.

1. What is the diagnosis?
2. List 4 steps in her management.

Question 10

A 24 year old secretary visits her GP to discuss a number of personal problems. She has noticed that her periods have become irregular and that she is developing coarse hairs over her breasts, upper lip and chin.

On examination she is hirsute with marked facial acne. Her blood pressure is 150/95mm.Hg She has cliteromegaly.

She is feeling very depressed and requests the mini pill as she has heard that this will improve all her problems.

Her GP refers her for investigations and she is found to have:

Investigations:

Prolactin	324 mu/l (<480 mu/l)
LH	8 iu/l (2-9 iu/l follicular, 1-13 luteal iu/l)
FSH	9 iu/l (1-10 iu/l follicular,2-9 luteal iu/l)
Testosterone	8.1 (0.5-2.5 nmol/l)
Androstenedione	9 mmol/l (4-11 mmol/l)
DHEAS	17.2 mmol/l (0.7-11.5 mmol/l)

1. What is the diagnosis?
2. What investigation would assist you with confirming the diagnosis?

Question 11

One week following heart transplantation, a 45 year old man develops bruising and oliguria. Investigations reveal:

Hb	8.2 g/dl
WCC	12 x 10⁹/l
Platelets	16 x 10⁹/l
Blood film:	schistocytes
	Burr Cells
PT	normal
APTT	normal
Sodium	130 mmol/l
Potassium	5.1 mmol/l
Urea	30.1 mmol/l
Creatinine	590 µmol/l
Alk Phos	85 iu/l
ALT	34 iu/l
Bilirubin	90 µmol/l
Cultures	negative

1. What is the diagnosis?
2. What is the likely cause?
3. What is the therapy indicated?

Question 12

A 60 year old man with adult polycystic kidney disease and stable renal impairment presents with a 1 month history of left loin pain, polydipsia and polyuria. Investigations are as follows:

Hb	11.3 g/dl
WCC	7.2 x 10⁹/l
Platelets	300 x 10⁹/l
Sodium	135 mmol/l
Potassium	4.2 mmol/l
Bicarbonate	17 mmol/l
Urea	40 mmol/l
Creatinine	390 µmol/l
Calcium	3.3 mmol/l
Albumin	37 g/l
Alk Phos	210 iu/l
Glucose	6.5 mmol/l
Urinalysis	blood +++, protein +
AXR	Normal
CXR	(Figure A)

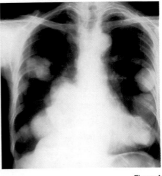

Figure A

1. What is the diagnosis?
2. What 2 investigations would you perform?
3. Give two explanations for the haemoglobin concentration.
4. What is the explanation for the abnormal chest x-ray?

Question 13

A 30 year old Afro-Caribbean woman presents with severe loin pain.

Investigations:

Sodium	138 mmol/l
Potassium	2.5 mmol/l
Urea	4.0 mmol/l
Creatinine	120 μmol/l
Chloride	115 mmol/l
Urinary pH	6.3
Anion gap	11
pCO_2	4 kPa

1. What is the serum bicarbonate concentration?
2. What is the diagnosis, and the most likely aetiology?
3. What is the cause of the loin pain?

Question 14

A 40 year old lady presents to clinic with dysuria and frequency.
She is diagnosed with a urinary tract infection and prescribed antibiotics.
A week later she is seen with nausea and vomiting.

Investigations:

Sodium	135 mmol/l
Potassium	4.5 mmol/l
Bicarbonate	21 mmol/l
Urea	6.1 mmol/l
Creatinine	190 μmol/l

1. What is the likely explanation for the above?

Question 15

A 70 year old man presents with lethargy and nausea. On examination his blood pressure is 190/110 mm.Hg and he has a palpable globular mass above the symphysis pubis.

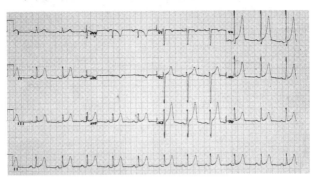

Figure A

Investigations:

Hb	7 g/dl
MCV	90 fl
WCC	8.5 x 10⁹/l
Platelets	400 x 10⁹/l
Urea	40 mmol/l
Creatinine	1000 µmol/l
ECG	(Figure A)

1. What is the abnormality on the ECG?
2. What 4 urgent measures should be taken?

Question 16

A 22 year old woman was well until 12 months ago, when she started to develop shortness of breath associated with chest tightness. There was no previous history of cyanosis, congenital heart disease or rheumatic fever. She did not smoke or drink alcohol. Her mother was alive and healthy but her father had died suddenly 10 years ago. Her brother and sister were alive and well.

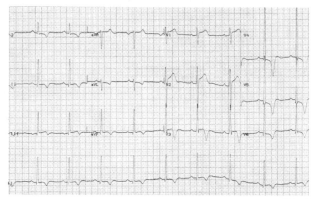

Figure A

On clinical examination she was not clubbed or anaemic. The pulse was 80 beats per minute and regular with normal character. Blood pressure was 120/70 mm.Hg and the JVP was not elevated. The cardiac apex was not displaced but had a double impulse. Cardiac auscultation revealed a normal first and second heart sound with an additional fourth heart sound and a soft late systolic murmur at the apex. Remainder of the examination was unremarkable.

Investigations:

Hb	12 g/dl
WCC	5.6×10^9/l
Platelets	350×10^9/l
Lipid profile	Normal
CXR	Normal
ECG	(Figure A)

1. What is the diagnosis?
2. What tests would you perform and what would you expect to see?
3. How would you treat the patient's symptoms?

Question 17

A 50 year old woman was brought into casualty having been found collapsed on the floor of her flat. She had the following blood test results:

Investigations:

Sodium	135 mmol/l
Potassium	7.1 mmol/l
Urea	20 mmol/l
Creatinine	750 µmmol/l
Calcium	1.9 mmol/l
Albumin	40 g/l
AST	99 u/l
Alk Phos	130 iu/l
GGT	110 iu/l
Hb	10 g/dl
WCC	13 x 10^9/l
Urinalysis	blood +++
Red cell transketolase	low

1. What is the diagnosis?
2. Give 2 potential causes in this case.

A 33 year old woman attends the medical out-patient clinic with a one month history of fatigue, constipation and weight gain of 7kg. On examination there is mild ankle oedema. She undergoes blood tests which are as follows:

Investigations:

Hb	9 g/dl
WCC	10 x 10^9/l
Platelets	252 x 10^9/l
MCV	102 fl
Albumin	38 g/l
Urea	4.0 mmol/l
Creatinine	120 μmol/l
Alk.Phos	170 iu/l
Calcium	2.38 mmol/l
Phosphate	1.0 mmol/l
T4	200 nmol/l (70-160 nmol/l)
TSH	1.5 mu/l (0.8-3.5 mu/l)

1. What one test would you request?
2. What is the diagnosis?

A 60 year old woman presents with pain over both iliac crests for the past 2-3 months. She had been taking ibuprofen to relieve this pain on an intermittent basis. More recently she had been complaining of nausea, abdominal discomfort and constipation. In the last week she had noticed a progressive loss of vision in her left eye.

Investigations:

Sodium	134 mmol/l
Potassium	4.9 mmol/l
Urea	13.5 mmol/l
Creatinine	189 μmol/l
Albumin	24 g/l
Calcium	3.1 mmol/l
24 hour urine	5g
AXR	Faecal loading
Pelvic X-ray	(Figure A)
Left Fundus	(Figure B)
ECG	(Figure C)

Figure A

1. What is the most likely diagnosis?
2. What other tests would you carry out?
3. Why is this woman losing vision in her left eye?
4. What is the cause of the cardiac abnormality?
5. Comment on this patient's prognosis.

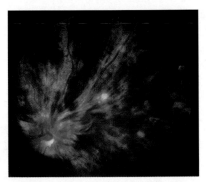

Figure B

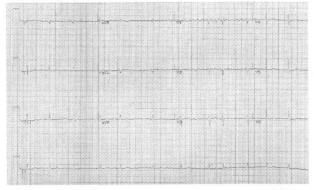

Figure C

18

Question 20

A 45 year old woman presents with a 3 week history of right knee pain and swelling. In the same period she also reports left upper quadrant pains and night sweats. On one night she noted blurring of one eye associated with confusion. On two occasions she had noted pre-syncope, both times while at rest. She was on no medication, had no past medical history of note or any significant family history.

On examination she was unwell and febrile with a temperature of 39.5°C. Her pulse was thready with a rate of 110 beats per minute. Blood pressure was 130/80 mm.Hg and respiratory rate was 30/minute. She had a tender nodule on her right index finger and fundoscopy of the right eye is shown in (Figure A). No bruits were audible. Her heart sounds demonstrated a systolic murmur and a short diastolic murmur at the left sternal edge. The peripheral pulses in the left foot were absent.

Investigations:

Hb	10 g/dl
WCC	12 x 10⁹/l
Platelets	600 x 10⁹/l
ESR	80 mm/hour

Sodium	136 mmol/l
Potassium	5 mmol/l
Creatinine	90 µmol/l

Albumin	29 g/l
Bilirubin	12 µmol/l
AST	56 iu/l
Alk Phos	155 iu/l
Calcium	2.1 mmol/l

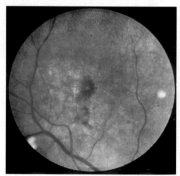

Figure A

Urine	protein ++; blood +	
ECHO	(Figure B)	
CXR	normal	

ABG	pO$_2$	10 kPa
	pCO$_2$	3.1 kPa
	HCO3	18 mmol/l
	BE−5.1	

1. What is the diagnosis? What is the aetiology?
2. What investigations are indicated?

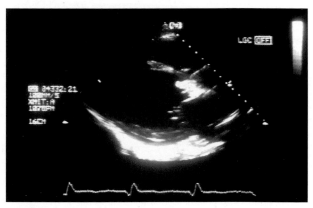

Figure B

Question 21

A 30 year old woman presents with dyspnoea on exertion and fatigue mainly in the evenings. She has a past history of hypothyroidism and was on thyroxine therapy. She had no other past medical problems and had no family history of any kind. She had been seen by her GP who had treated her for asthma without any success.

On examination she had slurred speech and appeared sleepy. There was no clubbing, anaemia or oedema. Cardiovascular, respiratory and abdominal examination was completely normal. Neurological examination revealed normal papillary reflexes, normal cranial nerves, no sensory deficit or pyramidal signs.

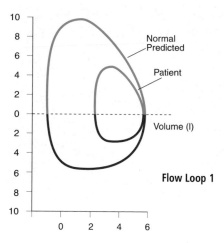

Flow loop on admission.

Investigations:

CXR	Normal	
VQ scan	Normal	
Resting ABG	pO$_2$	6.0 k/Pa
	pCO$_2$	9.0 k/Pa

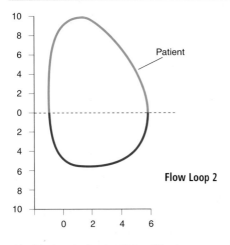

Flow Loop 2

After injection of a drug her ABG and flow loop were repeated
10 minutes later.

pO$_2$	11.0 k/Pa
pCO$_2$	4.5 k/Pa

1. What is the diagnosis?
2. What group of muscles is most commonly affected?
3. What drug was administered?
4. What other tests would you request?
5. What treatment is required?

Question 22

A 21 year old man is admitted with a 1 week history of fever, sore throat, and abdominal pain. He has just returned from a holiday on the Costa del Sol. He has cervical lymphadenopathy and pharyngeal examination reveals a purulent exudate. On abdominal examination he has 3cm splenomegaly.

Investigations:

Hb	10 g/dl
WCC	13 x 10⁹/l
Platelets	290 x 10⁹/l
Blood film	(Figure A)
ESR	56 mm/hour
Albumin	39 g/l
Alk Phos	188 iu/l
ALT	200 iu/l
Bilirubin	88 μmol/l

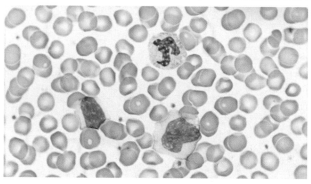

Figure A

1. What is the diagnosis in this case?
2. What does the blood film show? Give four causes of this.
3. What test would you perform to confirm the diagnosis?

A 65 year old man was seen in casualty with progressive shortness of breath on exertion and a dry cough over the last 3-4 months. He had also noticed swelling of his ankles. His general practitioner had prescribed frusemide without any beneficial effect. Ten years ago he had undergone coronary artery bypass grafting to three vessels following worsening angina. His other medication included aspirin and omeprazole.

On examination he was warm but not febrile. He had peripheral cyanosis and his pulse was 78 beats per minute and irregularly irregular. His blood pressure was 130/75 mm.Hg and his respiratory rate was 25/minute. He had an elevated JVP. Heart sounds were normal with a parasternal heave. His chest examination revealed inspiratory crackles at both bases and midzones.

Investigations:

Hb	16 g/dl
WCC	9 x 10⁹/l
Platelets	388 x 10⁹/l
ESR	78 mm/hour
Sodium	136 mmol/l
Potassium	4.6 mmol/l
Urea	10 mmol/l
Creatinine	100 µmol/l
Protein	78 g/l
Albumin	40 g/l
ALT	50 iu/l
Alk Phos	190 iu/l
Bilirubin	29 µmol/l
ANA	positive
Rheumatoid Factor	1/160
CXR	(Figure A)

Figure A

ECG	AF with RBBB
Echo	Normal LV function
FEV1	60%
FVC	55%
pO_2	8.2 kPa
pCO_2	3.5 kPa

1. What is the cause of this patient's breathlessness?
2. What 2 other investigations would you carry out to confirm the diagnosis?

Question 24

A 21 year old man is referred to clinic with a history of palpitations, chest pain and syncope. He had a normal childhood and had no past medical history of note. He was on no medication and had no family history of cardiac disease. He was a non-smoker and teetotal. The chest pains were sharp in nature and not related to exertion. He had suffered one bout of syncope while walking to work.

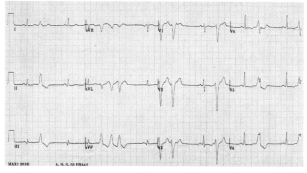

Figure A

Physical examination is unremarkable. Resting ECG (Figure A) is shown opposite. His echocardiogram shows mildly impaired left and right ventricular contractility with mild enlargement of the right ventricle. A 24-hour tape shows sinus rhythm throughout with frequent ventricular ectopics of LBBB morphology and few runs of non-sustained ventricular tachycardia. An ECG during an episode of palpitation is shown in (Figure B).

1. Comment on the ECG in figure A.
2. What is the diagnosis?
3. What other tests would you request to confirm diagnosis?

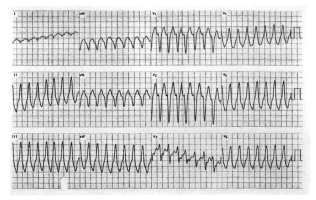

Figure B

A 39 year old woman complains of dyspnoea. She undergoes cardiac catheterisation which reveals the following data.

Investigations:

	Sat %O2	Pressure (mm.Hg)
RA	74	Mean 5
		A-wave 11
RV	76	65/0-9
PA	75	33/12
PCWP		Mean 30
		A-wave = 33
LV	99	115/0-10
Aorta	98	115/75

1. Describe the primary cardiac lesions.
2. What rhythm is the patient in?

Question 26

A 31 year old woman presented with a three week history of intermittent upper abdominal pain and vomiting. On the day of admission she had a bowel motion with loose watery stool. There was no blood or mucus in the stool. She had a past medical history of ulcerative colitis which was diagnosed at the age of 14 years and was stable on Sulphasalazine. In the past she had received two courses of steroids for acute exacerbation of her colitis but had never completed them. Her only other drug history was that she was currently on the contraceptive pill. She had been married for 6 years and had two children aged 5 and 3 years. She smoked 10 cigarettes per day and consumed one or two units of alcohol per week.

On examination she appeared unwell. Her tongue was dry and there was loss of skin turgor. She had mild lower limb pitting oedema. The heart rate was 98 beats per minute. The blood pressure was 100/65 mm.Hg. The temperature was 36.8°C. The abdomen was slightly distended and there was generalised tenderness. The liver was palpable three finger breadths below the costal margin but was no evidence of a palpable spleen or any other palpable masses in the abdomen. Percussion of the abdomen revealed shifting dullness.

Rectal examination was normal.

Examination of the respiratory and cardiovascular system was normal.

Investigations:

Hb	13 g/dl
WCC	8 x 10⁹/l
Platelets	190 x 10⁹/l
Sodium	131 mmol/l
Potassium	3.1 mmol/l
Urea	7.2 mmol/l
Creatinine	100 µmol/l
Bilirubin	20 µmol/l
AST (SGPT)	24 iu/l
ALT (SGOT)	21 iu/l
Alk phos	120 iu/l
Albumin	29 g/l
CXR	Normal heart size. Clear lung fields.

1. What two investigations would you request to ascertain the cause of the presentation?
2. What two underlying diagnoses would you consider in this patient

Question 27

A 34 year old man with haemophilia A was admitted with a painful, swollen right knee. He had a past history of several admissions with recurrent lower limb haemarthroses which had responded well to factor VIII concentrates. He also had a history of essential hypertension which was controlled with Bendrofluazide and Propranolol. His serum was negative for HIV antigen, Hep Bs antigen and HCV antibody. He received factor VIII concentrate with improvement in the swelling over the first four days. On the fifth day he complained of severe pain in the right knee. On examination the knee was swollen and tender. He had a temperature of 38.1°C.

Investigations:

FBC	Hb	13.4 g/dl
	WCC	$14 \times 10^9/l$
	Platelets	$200 \times 10^9/l$
ESR		40 mm/h

1. Which of the following investigations would you request next?

A. Blood cultures
B. Factor VIII assay
C. Factor VIII antibody assay
D. Serum urate
E. Ultrasound of the knee

Question 28

A 65 year old woman with a history of branch occlusion of the central retinal vein complicated by glaucoma four years previously presented with reduced vision in the left eye. On examination the visual acuity in the left eye was 6/36 and in the right eye was 6/6. Her glaucoma was being treated with Timolol eye drops. Examination of the fundi demonstrated changes consistent with a branch retinal vein occlusion in the left eye. There was no optic atrophy. A MRI scan of the head was performed which is shown in Figure A.

1. Describe the abnormality on the MRI scan.
2. Which investigation would be therapeutically useful?

A. Plasma prolactin
B. Plasma gonadotrophins
C. Plasma TSH
D. Plasma ADH
E. Plasma cortisol

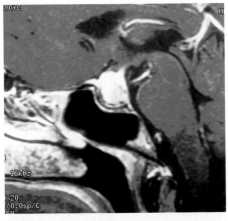

Figure A

Question 29

A 21 year old woman presented with a six week history of fever, general malaise and headaches. One week prior to admission she had an episode of loss of consciousness which was accompanied by urinary incontinence and transient weakness of the left hand.

On examination she was drowsy and there was rigidity of neck movements. She had a temperature of 38.4°C. The blood pressure was 120/80 mm.Hg. There were no focal neurological signs. On inspection of the oral cavity there were white plaques over the tonsils and the pharynx. Examination of the heart, lungs and abdomen was normal.

Investigations:

CT Scan brain	Normal	
Lumbar puncture	CSF opening pressure	230 mm H$_2$O
	Cells	120/mm^3 (all lymphocytes)
	Protein	1.4 g/l
	Glucose	1.4 mmol/l
	Gram stain	Negative
	ZN stain	Negative
Blood glucose		5.1 mmol/l

1. Which of the following investigations would be helpful in reaching a rapid diagnosis in this patient?

A. CSF protein immunoelectrophoresis
B. Indian ink stain on CSF
C. CSF ELISA for TB antigen
D. CSF pyruvate estimation
E. Blood cultures

Question 30

A 15 year old Nigerian girl was admitted with right upper quadrant abdominal pain. She had a history of sickle cell anaemia and had several admissions with hand and foot crises. During the last two admissions she complained of abdominal pain. She was born in England. She was the only child of a middle class family.

On examination she was distressed with pain. The temperature was 38. 4°C. She was mildly jaundiced. The pulse was 105 beats per minute and the blood pressure was 110/75 mm.Hg. On examination of the respiratory system there was dullness to percussion on the anterior aspect of the right lung. Abdominal examination revealed tenderness in the right upper quadrant. The liver was palpable 3 cm below the costal margin.

Investigations:

FBC	Hb	6 g/dl
	WCC	$12 \times 10^9/l$
	Platelets	$200 \times 10^9/l$
	Reticulocytes	17%
Urea/Electrolytes		Normal
Liver function	AST	50 iu/l
	Alk Phos	150 iu/l
	Albumin	34 g/l
Urinalysis	Urobilinogen	++
	Blood	0
	Protein	0
	Bilirubin	0
CXR		Opacification in the right upper zone

1. What is the cause of the abdominal pain?

2. What investigation would you request next?

3. What is the cause of the girl's respiratory and CXR findings?

Question 31

An 18 year old woman had a routine blood count in the first trimester of her pregnancy which was as follows:

Investigations:

FBC	Hb	10.5 g/dl
	WCC	5 x 10⁹/l
	Platelets	210 x 10⁹/l
	MCV	58 fl

Blood film	Numerous target cells
	Microcytosis
	Hypochromia

1. What two investigations would you perform to ascertain the cause of her anaemia?
2. What is the most probable diagnosis?

The following is a 12 lead ECG from an 18 year old boy who had undergone a surgical repair for a heart condition 10 years ago (Figure A).

1. Which two abnormalities can you detect on the ECG?

A. Complete right bundle branch block
B. Left bundle branch block
C. Left anterior hemiblock
D. Left posterior hemiblock
E. Dextrocardia
F. First degree AV block
G. Right ventricular hypertrophy
H. Left ventricular hypertrophy
I. Wolff-Parkinson White type A

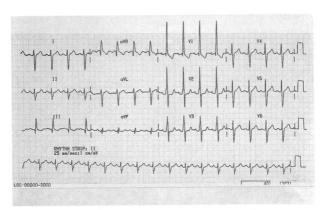

Figure A

Question 33

A 14 year old boy was admitted with haematemesis. Upper gastrointestinal endoscopy revealed oesophageal varices. On examination there were no peripheral stigmata of chronic liver disease but there was a palpable spleen 4cm. below the costal margin.

Invasive venous pressures were as follows.

Hepatic wedge pressure	6 mm. Hg (Normal < 7)
Inferior vena cava	3 mm. Hg (Normal < 5)

1. What is the diagnosis?
2. What investigation would you perform to confirm the diagnosis?

Question 34

A 65 year old man was admitted with an acute myocardial infarction and received Streptokinase. Twelve hours later he became nauseous and was noted to have a bradycardia (Figure A).

1. What is the cause of the Bradycardia.
2. What is the next management step?

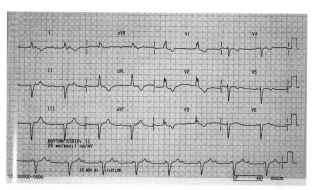

Figure A

A 64 year old man is investigated for breathlessness.
Respiratory function tests are as follows -

Investigations:

	% Predicted
FEV (l/min)	50%
FVC(l/min)	75%
TLC	124%
KCO	43%

1. What diagnosis are the abnormalities consistent with?

A 32 year old woman presents with general malaise, easy bruising and joint pains.
On examination she had a palpable spleen.

Investigations:

FBC	Hb	10 g/dl
	WCC	2.2×10^9/l (neutrophils 1.5×10^9/l)
	Platelets	46×10^9/l
ESR		80 mm/h

1. What is the diagnosis?

A 94 year old woman with a history of asthma was admitted with increasing breathlessness and chest tightness. On examination she was anxious and auscultation of the lung fields revealed a clear chest. Her medication comprised of one Frumil tablet per day and a regular Salbutamol inhaler.

Investigations:

Biochemistry	Sodium	124 mmol/l
	Potassium	3.2 mmol/l
	Urea	7.4 mmol/l
	Creatinine	80 μmol/l

Arterial blood gases	pH	7.46
(on air)	pO_2	11.4 kPa
	pCO_2	3.2 kPa
	Bicarbonate	29 mmol/l
	O_2 Saturation	99%

1. What is the metabolic abnormality in this patient?

A. Compensated respiratory alkalosis.

B. Uncompensated respiratory alkalosis.

C. Metabolic alkalosis.

D. Respiratory and metabolic alkalosis.

E. Metabolic acidosis.

2. Give two explanations for the metabolic abnormality?

A 62 year old woman complained of pain and tingling in her left arm which was worsened on hanging up the washing.

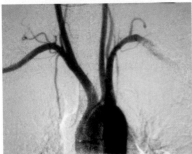

Figure A

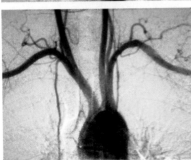

Figure B

Aortic arch angiography with the arms up (Figure A) and arms down (Figure B).

1. What is the diagnosis?

Question 39

A young homosexual male with HIV infection was admitted with breathlessness. Due to an allergy to Septrin, he was treated with a combination of Dapsone and Trimethoprim for a putative diagnosis of Pneumocystis carinii pneumonia. On the third day of treatment he became more breathless and appeared cyanosed.

Investigations:

Arterial blood gases	pH	7.4 mmol/l
(on 40% Oxygen)	pO$_2$	4.6 kPa
	pCO$_2$	4.2 kPa
	Bicarbonate	19 mmol/l
	O$_2$ Saturation	85%

1. Which investigation would you perform to determine the cause of his cyanosis?

Question 40

A 52 year old homeless male was admitted to the Casualty department looking very ill.

Investigations:

Electrolytes	Sodium	125 mmol/l
	Potassium	2.4 mmol/l
	Chloride	56 mmol/l
	Urea	39 mmol/l
	Creatinine	180 μmol/l
	Bicarbonate	48 mmol/l

1. What is the most probable explanation for these blood results?

A 70 year old man was awoken with retrosternal chest pain radiating into his left arm in the early hours of the morning. The pain was persistent for 5 hours and unrelieved by taking antacids before finally subsiding. The following day he consulted his daughter over the telephone who persuaded him to make an urgent appointment with his general practitioner. There was a past history of mild hypertension and hypothyroidism. The latter was diagnosed over a year ago after the patient presented with lethargy and was treated with 25µg of thyroxine, however, the drug was stopped by the patient within three months because he felt well again. He was a non smoker and consumed alcohol on a very infrequent basis.

Over the past two months he had felt lethargic again and complained of headaches and visual problems. He had not been sleeping very well and saw another doctor who diagnosed depression. He lived alone. He had been widowed three years previously. He took antacids for infrequent indigestion.

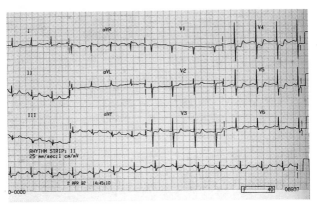

Figure A

On visiting his general practitioner an ECG was performed (Figure A). He was referred to the local hospital immediately for further evaluation. On arrival to the hospital he appeared pale but was well perfused. His heart rate was 50 beats per minute and the blood pressure was 150/95 mm.Hg. The heart sounds were normal and the chest was clear. There was no clinical evidence of cardiac failure. Neurological examination revealed abnormal visual fields (Figure B). Pubic and axillary hair was scarce. These findings prompted a skull X-ray (Figure C).

Further investigations:

FBC	Hb	9.6 g/dl	
	WCC	4 x 10⁹/l	
	Platelets	150 x 10⁹/l	
MCV		108 fl	
Biochemistry	Sodium	132 mmol/l	
	Potassium	3.8 mmol/l	
	Urea	3 mmol/l	

	Day 1	Day 3
Creatinine phosphokinase	300 u/l	170 u/l
Lactate dehydrogenase (NR 240-550)	300 u/l	600 u/l

TSH	21 nmol/l
Thyroxine	30 nmol/l
Thyroid microsomal antibodies	Positive 1/3000
Morning cortisol	200 ng/l
Leutinizing hormone	0.5 u/l (NR 1-10units/l)
Follicle stimulating hormone	0.4 u/l (NR 1-7units/l)
Prolactin	550 mu/l (< 480 mu/l)

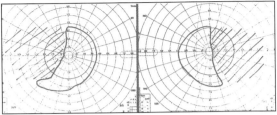

Figure B

1. List the abnormalities on the ECG.

2. Give two reasons for the elevated creatinine phosphokinase.

3. List three abnormalities on the skull X-ray.

4. What is the abnormality on the visual fields?

5. What is the most likely cause of the abnormal thyroid function tests?

6. Which further investigation is required?

7. What is the underlying endocrine diagnosis?

8. Which 2 investigations would you perform to investigate the cause of his anaemia?

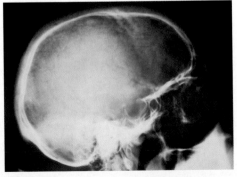

Figure C

Question 42

A 29 year old man presented to Casualty with a sudden onset of severe chest pain radiating between his shoulders which was not associated with shortness of breath. His father had a heart murmur and died prematurely. His brother also had a heart murmur but was alive and well.

On examination he was distressed. He was tall, thin and kyphotic. Heart rate was 115 beats per minutes and blood pressure was 185/65 mmHg. Heart sounds were normal but there was an audible early diastolic murmur at the left lower sternal edge. Auscultation of the lung fields revealed reduced air entry at the left lung base. An ECG done on admission revealed T wave inversion in leads I, aVl, V5 and V6.

1. What is the likely cause of his chest pain ?
2. Which single investigation would you request to confirm the cause of the chest pain ?
3. What is the underlying diagnosis ?

An 65 year old man was admitted with a six week history of progressive dyspnoea. One week before admission he had developed dyspnoea at rest, orthopnoea, paroxysmal nocturnal dyspnoea, loss of appetite and weight loss of over 3.14 kg. He had a cough productive of yellowish - brown sputum and on two occasions he had noticed bright red sputum. His general practitioner had prescribed Frusemide 40mg daily which he had taken for 6 weeks, with transient relief of his symptoms initially. The patient had enjoyed a very active and independent life and, apart from a truncal vagotomy and drainage procedure for a perforated duodenal ulcer 30 years ago, he had been very well. He was a non-smoker.

On examination he appeared pale and was dyspnoeic. The heart rate was 144 beats per minute and irregularly irregular. The BP was 160/100 mm.Hg. The JVP was not raised, respiratory rate was 30/minute and temperature was 38°C. Heart sounds appeared

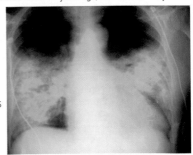

Figure A

normal; there were no audible murmurs. Auscultation of the lung fields revealed fine inspiratory crackles anteriorly only. Examination of the abdomen and central nervous system was normal. A subclavian line was inserted. CVP was 3cm H20. A urinary catheter drained a residual of 300ml of urine.

Investigations:

FBC	Hb	5.3 g/dl
	WCC	$17 \times 10^9/l$
	Platelets	$249 \times 10^9/l$
	MCV	89 fl
	MCHC	34 g/dl
ESR		82 mm/hour

Sodium	131 mmol/l	
Potassium	5.7 mmol/l	
Urea	40 mmol/l	
Creatinine	700 µmol/l	
Calcium	2.0 mmol/l	
Phosphate	0.9 mmol/l	
Albumin	33 mmol/l	
LFTs	Normal	
TFTs	Normal	
CRP	316 g/l	
PT	12 seconds	(control 12 seconds)
PTTK	43 seconds	(control 41 seconds)

Investigations continued:

Arterial blood gases:		
pH	7.35	
pCO_2	5.1 kPa	
pO_2	6.7 kPa	
Bicarbonate	12 mmol/l	
O_2 Sat	72%	
Blood cultures	x 2	Negative.
Urinalysis	Blood +++	
	Protein +++	
	Pus cells +++	
	Granular casts +++	
	No growth.	

| ECG | Fast atrial fibrillation with voltage criteria for LVH |

| CXR | (Figure A) |

Echocardiogram	Biatrial enlargement.
	Left ventricular hypertrophy with good systolic function.
	The mitral valve appeared normal.

| Renal ultrasound | Normal sized kidneys with echogenic renal parenchyma. |
| | No evidence of obstruction. |

The patient was treated with intravenous Cefuroxime and Erythromycin, rehydrated gently and transfused 3 units of packed cells.

The temperature came down, CVP increased to 9cm H_2O and urine output averaged 420ml / 24h. Hb following transfusion was 6.4 g/dl. Whilst on the ward the patient had 3 episodes of frank haemoptysis.

Serial chest X-rays over 4 days remained unchanged. He reverted to sinus rhythm 3 days after commencing Digoxin.

Serum biochemistry on day 4:

Sodium	131 mmol/l
Potassium	6.0 mmol/l
Urea	50 mmol/l
Creatinine	1060 µmol/l

1. List 2 possible diagnoses.

2. List 3 further tests which would be useful in confirming the diagnosis.

3. The patient was given 120mg of intravenous Frusemide with little increase in urine output. What would be the next step in your management?

These results are from a 56 year old woman with mild jaundice and pruritis.

Investigations:

Serum	Bilirubin	46 micromol/l
	Aspartate transaminase	51 iu/l
	Alkaline phosphatase	310 iu/l
	Total protein	78 g/l
	Albumin	35 g/l

1. What is the most likely diagnosis?

2. Which two tests would you perform to confirm the diagnosis?

A 26 year old lady complains of thirst and polyuria.

Investigations:

	POsm (mosmol/kg)	UOsm (mosmol/kg)
Basal	295	240
After 8 hours	305	250
Following DDAVP	760	20 mg intranasally

1. What is the diagnosis ?

2. Suggest three possible causes.

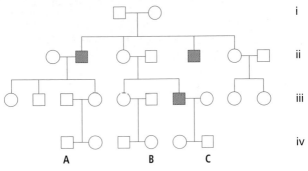

i

ii

iii

iv

A   B   C

Figure A

Above is a pedigree chart of a family with a bleeding disorder.

1. What is the mode of inheritance?
2. What is the chance of iv A being affected?
3. What is the chance of iv A being a carrier?
4. What is the chance of iv B being a carrier?
5. What is the chance of iv C being affected?

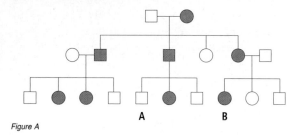

Figure A

1. What is the chance of A having an affected son?
2. What is the chance of B having an affected daughter?

Question 48

A 72 year old lady was admitted in a semi-comatosed state. According to her husband she was well until three months previously, following which she had become inattentive and had problems with short-term memory. She had become more introvert and had transformed from being a talkative lady to one who appeared almost "mute" on some days. Her GP had prescribed Amytriptilline 3 weeks previously without any effect. On the day of admission her husband witnessed her collapse and noted her to be twitching all her limbs for about five minutes. Following this she was drowsy.

On examination she had a normal aphasia, evidence of extrapyramidal tremor, myoclonic jerks and bilateral upgoing plantars.

Whilst on the ward her conscious level fluctuated. She had a low grade fever of 37°C. She complained of troublesome spasms affecting her legs.

Investigations:

Serum electrolyte and urea concentration	Normal
Serum liver tests	Normal
Full blood count	Normal
Plasma glucose	4.5 mmol/l
Serum corrected calcium	2.3 mmol/l
Urine/blood cultures	No growth
CT brain scan	Normal
CSF Analysis	
- pressure	100 mm H_2O
- protein	0.3 g/l
- glucose	4.0 mmol/l
- microscopy	No cells
- culture	No growth
Electroencephalogram (EEG)	Diffuse periodic slow wave and spike discharges.

1. What is the most likely diagnosis?

2. What further invasive investigation is occasionally required?

A 66 year old retired plumber was seen in the Casualty department with progressively increasing dyspnoea and wheeze. He had been seen by his general practitioner over one week previously and treated with antibiotics for a chest infection. According to his wife his appetite had been reduced and he had lost at least 6 kg in weight over the past month. He stopped smoking five years previously and had worked as a docker for fifteen years.

On examination he appeared thin and tachypnoeic. There was no clinical evidence of cyanosis or clubbing. He had a hoarse voice. Respiratory examination revealed reduced chest expansion of the left hemithorax and dullness to percussion with reduced air entry affecting the left anterior hemithorax.

A chest radiograph revealed left upper lobe collapse; left pleural effusion; alveolar shadowing of the left middle and lower zones. There was a small radiolucent lesion in the 5th left rib.

The patient was given oral Amoxycillin and Erythromycin for one week and asked to return for repeat CXR in two weeks, however, only four days later he was admitted as an emergency with increasing confusion and dehydration. According to his wife he had been extremely thirsty and was waking several times each night to pass large volumes of urine.

Investigations:

FBC	Hb	10.8 g/dl
	WCC	14.2 x 10^9/l
	Platelets	80 x 10^9/l
	MCV	91 fl

Blood film shows myelocytes and occasional normoblasts

Flow loop curve (Figure A)

U&E	Sodium	133 mmol/l
	Potassium	3.9 mmol/l
	Urea	18 mmol/l
	Creatinine	179 µmmol/l
Glucose		8.1 mmol/l
Urinalysis	glucose	Nil.
	ketones	+

1. What is the probable underlying diagnosis ?

2. What are the two abnormalities on the flow loop curve?

3. Give two possible reasons for his confusion.

4. What is the most likely reason for his polydipsia and polyuria ?

5. Give two reasons why this man is incurable.

6. Give four immediate treatment strategies.

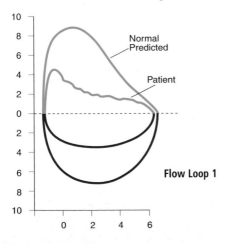

Flow Loop 1

A 4 year old boy was admitted with lethargy and easy bruising. His blood film is shown below (Figure A).

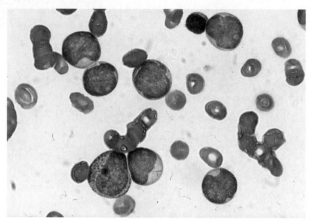

Figure A

1. What is the diagnosis?

Answers

Answer 1

1. The most likely diagnosis is Cushing's syndrome although depression, alcohol and obesity may all mimic the syndrome. Depression is also a common symptom of Cushing's syndrome.

2. Insulin tolerance test with measurement of blood glucose and Cortisol.

   Alcohol as a cause for this man's symptoms can be excluded by the normal γGT. Both Cushing's syndrome and depression are associated with a loss of cortisol circadian rhythm hence blood samples taken for ACTH and cortisol at 9.00am and 6.00pm are not indicated here. Similarly both conditions will give a raised plasma random cortisol, raised urinary 17-Oxogenic corticosteroids and will not be associated with a failure to suppress plasma cortisol during a 48 hour dexamethasone suppression test.

   In depression, the cortisol response to hypoglycaemia is intact. For an adequate stimulus, the blood glucose must fall below 2.2mmol. The cortisol response to hypoglycaemia is lost in Cushing's syndrome.

Common features of Cushing's syndrome:	Aetiology of Cushing's syndrome:
Central obesity (90%)	*ACTH dependent* (84%)
Hypertension (85%)	1. Pituitary (Cushing's disease)
Glucose intolerance (80%)	2. Ectopic
Plethoric facies (80%)	
Purple striae (65%)	*Non ACTH dependent* (16%)
Hirsutism (65%)	1. Adrenal adenoma/carcinoma
Menstrual disturbances (60%)	
Bruising (40%)	*Iatrogenic*
	Glucocorticoid therapy
Less common features include mental disturbances, pigmentation, acne and hypokalaemic alkalosis.	*Pseudo-Cushing's* alcohol, depression

Answer 2

1. TB Meningitis

   Cryptococcal Meningitis

   Other possible causes are tabulated below

Causes of CSF Lymphocytosis high protein & low glucose
TB
Cryptococcus
Cerebral malignancy
Brucella
Listeria
Lyme disease
Cerebral abscess
Cerebral malaria

2. Ziehl-Neelsen stain for TB.

   Indian ink stain for Cryptococcus.

Answer 3

1. Ectopic ACTH production by a bronchial carcinoma.

The whole body venous sampling demonstrates a mediastinal tumour secreting ACTH.

The chest X-ray does not reveal any obvious abnormality.

This condition should be suspected where there is a short history, weight loss, pigmentation, a very high plasma ACTH, severe myopathy and hypokalaemic alkalosis. Patients with Cushing's disease are less likely to manifest a hypokalaemic alkalosis (10%) in comparison to Ectopic ACTH driven Cushing's (80%).

Whole body venous sampling is indicated when ACTH dependent Cushing's is suspected but the tumour has not been identified by detailed radiology.

Answer 4

1. Subacute thyroiditis
2. Radioiodine scan. The thyroid radioactive iodine uptake is always suppressed usually to less than 3% in 24 hours. This is due to disruption of the iodine trapping mechanism caused by inflammation.
3. Aspirin 600mg QDS. Prednisolone 10-20mg OD for 1 week if pain is severe and not responding to aspirin.

Antithyroid drugs are not indicated.

Answer 5

1. He has diabetes and hypergonadotrophic hypogonadism.
2. Klinefelter's syndrome.

Klinefelter's syndrome occurs in 1/500 males.
The underlying abnormality is the presence of an extra X chromosome (47XXY).
The condition usually presents in adolescence and is characterised by varying degrees of sexual immaturity although many cases are not diagnosed earlier in life due to fears or denial by patients that there may be a problem.
These patients have small genitalia and testes and a slightly lower IQ.
There is an increased risk of thyroid disorders, diabetes mellitus and breast cancer in these patients.

Answer 6

1. Plasma 25-Hydroxycholecalciferol, X-ray hips
   PTH
2. Osteomalacia
   This lady is from India and is a vegetarian.
   Her symptoms improve on return to India due to exposure to sunlight.

1. Primary Hyperaldosteronism
2. Paired renin and aldosterone levels when patient is ambulatory and 4 hours post recumbency.
   CT scan adrenal glands.

Answer 8

1. Fabrys disease. This is an x-linked disorder due to deficiency of the enzyme α-galactosidase
2. Skin or bone biopsy will demonstrate lipid inclusions and capillary dilatation.
   Assay for α-galactosidase A in leucocytes or cultured fibroblasts
3. Pain relief with carbamazepine/phenytoin or low dose opiate
   Renal dialysis
   Pulsed dye lazer therapy for cutaneous lesions

Answer 9

1. HELLP syndrome (heamolysis, elevated liver enzymes, low platelets) which is believed to be a more severe counterpart of the pre-eclamptic disorder.
   Heamolysis is characteristic with LDH raised > 600U/L.
   Platelet numbers have been useful to assess the disease severity.
   The symptoms of HELLP are often vague, hence the average delay in reaching the correct diagnosis is 8 days.

2. **a** Steroids   **b** Renal dialysis
   c Fresh frozen plasma   **d** Diazipam for epilepsy

   Use of intravenous dexamethasone is associated with a shorter duration of disease, faster recovery and reduced morbidity.

1. Virising androgen producing adrenal tumour.
   She has a short history of symptoms that are in keeping with
   hyperandrogenism.
   DHEAS is an adrenal androgen which would exclude ovarian pathology.
2. CT adrenals would assist in locating the tumour for surgical extraction .

1. Haemolytic uraemic syndrome caused by Cyclosporin A which is standard
   immunosuppression following cardiac transplantation.
2. The causes of HUS in childhood include infections such as E.Coli
   (VTEC O157:H7). In adults causes include pregnancy, HIV infection,
   carcinomas, chemotherapy and other drugs such as Cyclosporin A and
   Mitomycin.
   In adults HUS carries a poor prognosis with a mortality of 20-60%.
   The therapy for mild HUS is supportive and removing any offending agents
   if possible.
3. Plasma exchange is usually recommended for patients with more severe
   anaemia and ARF requiring dialysis. Neither heparin nor thrombolytics are
   useful and may cause bleeding. Steroids or cytotoxics are also not
   beneficial. There is benefit reported with antioxidants but this needs to be
   confirmed in studies.

Answer 12

1. This is a case of a renal cell carcinoma, a recognised complication of APCKD.

2. The two investigations are renal ultrasound or CT scanning and renal angiography. The triad of loin pain, haematuria and renal mass can be due to APCKD alone. The clue in this case is the hypercalcaemia due to ectopic PTH-like substance. This is one of the paraneoplastic manifestations of a hypernephroma.

3. The haemoglobin concentration is inappropriately high for a patient with renal impairment and could be due to:

a. APCKD is associated with erythropoetin production

b. Ectopic erthyropoetin production is paraneoplastic feature of hypernephroma

c. Haemoconcentration due to dehydration resulting from hypercalcaemia.

4. Cannon ball metastases to the lung from the hypernephroma.

Answer 13

1. The bicarbonate concentration is 14.5 mmol/l. This is derived from the equation: Anion Gap = $(Na^+ + K^+) - (HCO3^- + Cl^-)$

2. The diagnosis is (distal) renal tubular acidosis type 1. The biochemical abnormality is of a normal anion gap hyperchloraemic metabolic acidosis. In this condition the distal renal tubule is unable to excrete protons causing inappropriately alkaline urine in the face of a metabolic acidosis.

3. Nephrocalcinosis and renal calculi are well-recognised complications of type 1 RTA. This is due to the alkaline urine precipitating oxalate salts forming stones.

The causes of type 1 RTA include hereditary, hypergammaglobulinaemia, sjörgen's syndrome, chronic active hepatitis, hyperparathyroidism, medullary sponge kidney, tubulo-interstitial disease, obstructive uropathy, sickle cell disease, chronic pyelonephritis and drugs (eg. Lithium, Amphoterecin).
The most probable aetiology of the RTA type 1 in this case is sickle cell disease.

Answer 14

1. The elevated creatinine is due to treatment with trimethoprim. True renal impairment is unlikely with a normal serum urea concentration. Trimethoprim competes with creatinine for excretion in the distal convoluted tubule.

Urea > Creatinine: Pre-renal failure (eg. Bleeding, Dehydration)
Steroids
Tetracyclines
Post-op
Acute-on-chronic renal failure

Creatinine > Urea: Liver disease
Rhabdomyolysis
Dialysis
Pregnancy

Trimethoprim

Answer 15

1. Tall T waves (i.e. T waves > 1.0mv) suggesting hyperkalaemia. ECG changes of hyperkalaemia become evident at a potassium concentration > 6.8 mmol/l.

2. **a.** Urinary catheterisation
   b. Intravenous calcium gluconate
   c. Intravenous dextrose (50 ml of 50% solution)
   d. Intravenous short-acting insulin (15-18 iu)

   The patient has end stage renal failure. The palpable bladder suggests this may be secondary to an obstructive atrophy. Treatment should be aimed at relieving the obstruction and treating the hyperkalaemia.

1. This young woman presents with angina at a young age without typical risk factors. There is a family history of sudden death suggesting a possible diagnosis of familial hypercholesterolaemia but the normal lipid profile is against this. The clinical signs are typical of hypertrophic cardiomyopathy (HCM). The ECG confirms left ventricular hypertrophy.

2. The diagnosis is confirmed by echocardiography which characteristically demonstrates hypertrophy of the left ventricle (typically in the septum; (Figure A)), systolic anterior motion of the mitral valve (SAM) and midsystolic closure of the aortic valve.

3. The mainstay of treatment of angina in HCM is with beta-blockers. They allow improved left ventricular filling and decrease outflow tract obstruction. Other therapeutic options include disopyramide and verapamil. Vasodilators should be used with caution in HCM with left ventricular out-flow obstruction. Significant symptomatic outflow obstruction can be treated using dual chamber pacing, alcohol septal ablation or myectomy. Risk assessment for sudden death is carried out using holter monitoring, exercise testing and patients at high risk are treated with either amiodarone or ICD's. First-degree relatives should be screened with ECG and echocardiography.

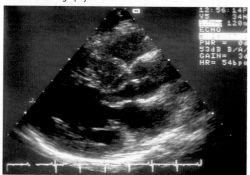

Figure A

1. The diagnosis is rhabdomyolysis.
2. The potential causes in this case are alcohol excess (elevated GGT and MCV, low red cell transketolase) and prolonged collapse from any cause.

Rhabdomyolysis is biochemically characterised by a disproportionate increase in creatinine from muscle necrosis and subsequent leak and elevation of muscle enzymes such as AST. There is also hyperkalaemia and hyperphosphataemia due to leak from necrotic muscle cells and hypocalcaemia due to binding of calcium by myoglobin released from damaged muscle.

Myoglobin produces reddish-brown discolouration of urine. Myoglobinuria gives a false positive urine dipstick for blood in the absence of true haematuria.

The treatment involves aggressive hydration and alkalinisation of the urine to minimise myoglobin-induced tubular damage and acute tubular necrosis.

A period of dialysis may however be required. Hypocalcaemia can be corrected by intravenous supplementation. Surgery to remove necrotic muscle tissue may be needed.

Answer 18

1. The test to request is a , β-hcg level or a pregnancy test.
2. The most likely diagnosis in a woman of this age with the above symptoms and biochemical abnormality is pregnancy. Although the clinical picture is compatible with a diagnosis of hypothyroidism the normal TSH rules this diagnosis out and the high total T4 is due to elevated concentrations of thyroid-binding globulin. The elevated MCV in pregnancy is due to relative folate deficiency as a result of high requirements.

Answer 19

1. The diagnosis is multiple myeloma complicated by severe hypercalcaemia and amyloidosis of the kidney and heart causing nephrotic syndrome and cardiac conduction abnormalities respectively.
2. The diagnosis can be confirmed by (1) examining the urine for Bence-Jones proteins (2) bone marrow examination for the presence of increased percentage of plasma cells (3) skeletal survey looking for osteolytic areas.
3. The cause of visual impairment in this case is central retinal vein occlusion secondary to hyperviscosity.
4. The patient has atrial fibrillation and small QRS complexes possibly secondary to infiltration of cardiac tissue by amyloid.
5. Poor prognostic indicators in myeloma include an elevated urea, hypercalcaemia, anaemia, a bone marrow plasma cell percentage of >10%, presence of β2-microglobulin and a paraprotein of greater than 40 g/l. This woman clearly has a poor prognosis.

Answer 20

1. The diagnosis is bacterial endocarditis of the aortic valve secondary to a septic arthritis of the knee. The most likely causative organism in this setting is Staphylococcus Aureus. The left upper quadrant pain is from splenomegaly secondary to splenic infarcts. The peripheral manifestations of bacterial endocarditis are due to thrombo-emboli (absent peripheral pulses) and immune complex deposition (Osler's nodes and Roth spots).
2. Serial blood cultures.

1. Myasthenia gravis. This disease is autoimmune in aetiology with antibodies against post-synaptic acetylcholine receptors having a pathogenic role. It is associated with other autoimmune disease such as thyroid disease and diabetes. A proportion of cases are associated with thymoma.

2. The commonest muscle groups affected are facial (ptosis, slurred speech) and shoulder girdle muscles but any muscle distribution can be involved. Involvement of respiratory muscles can lead to dyspnoea, respiratory failure or even sudden death.

3. Intravenous Edrophonium

4. The investigations indicated in this case include:
   (a) Fatiguability testing by repeated electrical stimulation of muscle groups
   (b) Correction of weakness by short-acting anti-cholinesterase such as edrophonium
   (c) Detection of antibodies to acetylcholine receptors
   (d) CT scan of chest/neck to check for thymoma
   (e) Thyroid antibody profile.
   (f) Demonstration of a paraprotein on serum immunoelectrophoresis

5. Treatment in severe cases involves steroids and plasmopheresis. Patients also require anticholinesterase drugs to augment muscle weakness.

   Thymic involvement is frequently seen in the form of hyperplasia and thymomas. The response to thymectomy is not predictable and current practice is to offer the operation to all patients with thymomas and severe disease.

Answer 22

1. The most likely diagnosis in this case is infectious mononucleosis complicated by hepatitis. The virus implicated is EBV, a member of the herpes viruses. Mild jaundice and biochemical hepatitis are common but clinical hepatitis is rare. The patient complains of sore throat, malaise and fever. Lymaphadenopathy and splenomegaly may be present.

2. Atypical lymphocytes
   Other causes of atypical lymphocytes include:
   CMV
   Toxoplasma
   Hepatitis A
   HIV
   Brucella

3. A Paul-Bunnell or Monospot test is usually positive and atypical lymphocytes are seen on the blood film (as in this case). Splenic rupture is a rare complication.

Answer 23

1. The diagnosis is cryptogenic fibrosing alveolitis.
   True exertional breathlessness, type 1 respiratory failure and restrictive lung defect support the diagnosis.
   The elevated JVP, AF and peripheral oedema may indicate early cor pulmonale.

2. Investigations indicated include:
   (1) Further pulmonary function tests including TLCO and KCO to demonstrate a reduction in gas transfer.
   (2) A lung biopsy to establish the diagnosis histologically.

   This condition is associated with other autoimmune diseases such as chronic active hepatitis (note mildly deranged LFT's), diabetes and thyroid disease.

Answer 24

1. The ECG demonstrates ventricular ectopics with LBBB morphology originating from the abnormal right ventricle. The patient also has T wave inversion in leads V1-V3. Inverted T waves in the right ventricular leads are common. Ectopy from the right ventrical (LBBB Morphology) is also common. Syncopy or sudden death may arise from ventricular tachycardia (Figure B) which also usually arises from the right ventrical and has a LBBB morphology.

2. The diagnosis is arrhythmogenic right ventricular cardiomyopathy (ARVC). This is suggested by the abnormal ECG in Figure A, the enlarged right ventrical and the ventricular tachycardia. This is a condition of uncertain origin characterised by fibro-fatty replacement of the right ventricular myocardium and less commonly may also involve the left ventricle. The pathology can either lead to electrical instability and subsequent ventricular arrhythmias, or to progressive heart failure.

3. Other tests indicated are right ventricular biopsy and MRI of the heart to look for abnormal fat deposition in the heart muscle.
   Therapy in ARVC involves suppression of ventricular arrhythmias using, β-blockers or amiodarone and preventing sudden death by using ICD's in high risk individuals. (eg. those with history of syncope) In the event of heart failure standard anti-failure therapy is used.

Answer 25

1. There is a gradient of 20 mm.Hg between the left atrial pressure and left ventricle pressure at end-diastole indicating mitral stenosis. The pulmonary valve is stenotic as there is a peak-to-peak pressure drop from the RV to the PA.

2. Due to the presence of the A-waves the rhythm must be sinus.

Answer 26

1. Liver ultrasound and Doppler studies
   Liver biopsy via internal jugular vein

   Also:
   Liver biopsy
   Hepatic venography
   Liver ultrasound
   Isotope liver scan
   Ascitic tap for cytology and protein estimation

   Ascitic tap

   Abdominal X-ray
   Urinary protein estimation

2. Hepatic vein thrombosis

   Carcinoma of the colon with hepatic metastases

   Chronic active hepatitis
   Cirrhosis of the liver

The patient has a long history of relatively quiescent ulcerative colitis and presents with a short history of intermittent upper abdominal pain, vomiting, tender hepatomegaly and ascites. There is no history of weight loss preceding the illness, however, she is a smoker and on the oral contraceptive pill, both of which are recognised risk factors for venous thrombosis. Ulcerative colitis itself is associated with an increased risk of venous thrombosis due to increased fibrinogen levels and the elevated plasma viscocity. The most likely diagnosis in this patient is hepatic vein thrombosis. Although portal vein thrombosis may also occur in ulcerative colitis, the abnormal liver function, and hepatomegaly would be against the diagnosis.

The differential diagnosis comprises carcinoma of the colon with hepatic metastases, chronic active hepatitis, cirrhosis of the liver and sclerosing cholangitis. Carcinoma of the colon is 10 times more common in a patient with long standing ulcerative colitis than in the general population, however, it is unusual for a patient with relatively well controlled colitis to present with extensive metastatic liver disease without a prodrome of ill health or bleeding per rectum. Sclerosing cholangitis is most often associated with ulcerative colitis but one would expect a much higher bilirubin level particularly if the associated cirrhosis was severe enough to cause hepatocellular failure as is suggested by the low albumin and ascites. Sclerosing cholangitis is most often associated with ulcerative colitis. Its prevalence is inversely related to the severity of colitis. Chronic active hepatitis is also recognised in ulcerative colitis but the normal transaminase level is against the diagnosis.

The investigation of choice is liver ultrasound with Doppler studies on hepatic venous flow. Liver biopsy and hepatic venography are also useful in making the diagnosis. A liver isotope scan may demonstrate preservation of the Riedel's lobe.

Some marks are awarded for investigation of the ascites. In malignant ascites cytology may be positive and the protein count is elevated. In ascites due to cirrhosis or hepatic failure the protein count is low.

Answer 27

A. Blood cultures

B. Factor VIII assay

C. Factor VIII antibody assay

D. Serum urate

E. Ultrasound of the knee

In a patient with haemophilia who has initially responded to factor VIII and subsequently develops pain and swelling in the knee associated with a fever and raised ESR it is mandatory to exclude septic arthritis. The investigation of choice would be blood cultures. Aspiration of the knee is avoided to prevent further haemarthrosis but may be undertaken with factor VIII cover if there is diagnostic difficulty regarding the presentation. Although it is possible to have acute gout in the knee, a serum urate level during an acute attack is rarely useful because it is often normal or low. The definitive test in gout is joint aspiration to look for negatively birefringent crystals under polarised light. Ultrasound of the knee would be unhelpful in distinguishing between blood and pus in the knee joint.

Answer 28

1. Large pituitary mass with evidence of suprasellar extension

   Pituitary tumour
   Enlarged pituitary mass

   Craniopharyngioma

   Prolactinoma
   Acidophil adenoma
   Meningioma
   Suprasellar cyst

2.

 A. Plasma prolactin
   B. Plasma gonadotrophins
   C. Plasma TSH
   D. Plasma ADH
   E. Plasma cortisol

An autonomous basophil pituitary adenoma secreting ACTH may cause hypertension and diabetes mellitus, both of which may have predisposed to branch central retinal vein occlusion, however such tumours are generally very small. Prolactin secreting or growth hormone secreting acidophil adenomas are usually large but pituitary tumours do not become large enough to compress the central retinal vein. Growth hormone secreting tumours may also cause hypertension and diabetes, however, growth hormone is not one of the options given above. A serum prolactin level would be most useful. An elevated level may indicate a macroprolactinoma in this case. Alternatively it may be suggestive of any large pituitary tumour with suprasellar extension causing compression of the hypophysis. In this case the opthalmological abnormality would be a coincidence rather than a consequence.

Answer 29

A. CSF protein immunoelectrophoresis

✓ B. Indian ink stain on CSF

C. CSF ELISA for TB antigen

D. CSF pyruvate estimation

E. Blood cultures

The patient has meningitis and focal neurological signs. The CSF demonstrates a lymphocytosis in association with a raised protein count and a low glucose. The differential diagnosis of such a CSF appearance includes tuberculosis, brucellosis, listerosis, crytococcal meningitis, CSF lymphoma and disseminated CSF malignancy. Blood cultures may be useful in the diagnosis of brucellosis but it is important to remember that the organism has been eradicated in cattle in this country. CSF immunoelectrophoresis is useful in the diagnosis of multiple sclerosis which does not constitute the differential diagnosis. CSF pyruvate estimation is useful in the diagnosis of mitochondrial encephalopathies. The options left include CSF ELISA for TB antigen and Indian ink stain which is used to diagnose cryptococcal meningitis. However, there is no available immunological test for the diagnosis of tuberculosis, therefore the best answer is Indian ink.

Cryptococcal meningitis affects immunosuppressed individuals and is a recognised complication of HIV infection. The white plaques over the tonsils and the pharynx in this patient suggest candida infection, however, oral candidiasis is not part of AIDS related complex.

Answer 30

1. Acute cholecystitis secondary to pigmented gall stones

2. Ultrasound of the liver

3. Right upper lobe pneumonia

Sickle cell anaemia is inherited as an autosomal recessive condition. A point mutation in the β globin gene leads to the substitution of glutamine by valine. In the deoxygenated state this leads to sickling of cells. Chronic low grade haemolysis is common. Sickle cell crises are due to occlusion of small vessels producing severe pain from affected organs. The bones are most commonly involved, particularly those of the digits of the hands and feet.

Precipitating factors for sickling include hypoxia, infection, dehydration, and pain. Chronic haemolysis predisposes to pigment gall stones which in turn predisposes to biliary colic and cholecystitis. Chronic infarction of the spleen predisposes these patients to infections with capsulated organisms, particularly Strep pneumoniae.

Sickle cell crises

1. Thrombotic (hand foot syndrome, abdominal pain, pulmonary infarction and strokes)
2. Haemolytic
3. Aplastic (Parvovirus may be the precipitating factor)
4. Sequestration (most fatal, usually in young children)

Answer 31

1. Haemoglobin electrophoresis
   Serum ferritin

   Marrow examination

2. ß-thalassaemia trait
   Iron deficiency

The MCV is disproportionately low compared with the haemoglobin.
This is typical of beta thalassaemia trait. In iron deficiency an MCV below 60
would be associated with a much lower haemoglobin. In iron deficiency the
serum ferritin is low. In ß-thalassaemia trait it may be raised due to impaired
iron utilisation by red cells.

Answer 32

A. Complete right bundle branch block
B. Left bundle branch block
C. Left anterior hemiblock
✔ D. Left posterior hemiblock
E. Dextrocardia
F. First degree AV block
✔ G. Right ventricular hypertrophy
H. Left ventricular hypertrophy
I. Wolff-Parkinson White type A

The patient has right axis deviation (left posterior hemiblock), partial RBBB
(QRS < 110 m.sec) and voltage criteria for right ventricular hypertrophy.

Answer 33

1. Portal vein thrombosis

   Splenic vein thrombosis

2. Liver ultrasound with Doppler flow studies

   Liver ultrasound

   Liver biopsy

The hepatic vein and inferior vena caval pressures are normal. Therefore the palpable spleen and the varices can only be explained by pre-hepatic portal hypertension i.e. portal vein thrombosis or splenic vein thrombosis.
A thrombosis in either of these veins will not affect liver function.
NOTE: The portal vein drains into the hepatic vein.

Answer 34

1. Complete heart block

2. Intravenous atropine followed by temporary pacing

Answer 35

1. Chronic obstructive airways disease (COAD)

The patient has an obstructive lung defect, gas trapping (increased TLC) and low transfer factor, all of which are consistent with chronic obstructive pulmonary disease.

1. Systemic lupus erythematosis

   Other possibilities include:
   Hodgkins lymphoma
   Non Hodgkins's lymphoma

   Aleukaemic leukaemia

Arthralgia, pancytopaenia and palpable spleen in a young woman should raise the possibility of SLE. Lymphoma is another possibility, particularly if the eosinophil count is relatively elevated. Felty's syndrome is associated with joint pains from rheumatoid arthritis and hypersplenism but is a feature of chronic rheumatoid disease. Post infectious thrombocytopenic purpura would not explain the low white cell count. It usually occurs in children and splenomegaly is rare.

1.
A. Compensated respiratory alkalosis
B. Uncompensated respiratory alkalosis
C. Metabolic alkalosis
✔ D. Respiratory and metabolic alkalosis
E. Metabolic acidosis

2. Hyperventilation and diuretic therapy explain the respiratory and metabolic alkalosis respectively.

1. The patient has a cervical rib which occludes the left subclavian artery during elevation of the left arm.

1. Methaemoglobin level

Also:

Sulphaemoglobin level

The oxygen tension is disproportionately low compared with the oxygen saturation. In the context of the question this is best explained by Dapsone induced methaemoglobinaemia. Methaemoglobin shifts the oxygen dissociation curve to the left. It binds oxygen avidly but does not release it to tissues, causing tissue hypoxia. Levels above 20% produce symptoms of breathlessness and headaches and levels above this may cause death.

Answer 40

1. Profuse vomiting

   Gastric outlet obstruction
   Pyloric stenosis

   Diuretic abuse

   Profound diarrhoea would not explain the very low chloride level.

Answer 41

1. ST segment depression in I, II, V3-V6
   Inverted T waves in aVl
   Sinus tachycardia.

2. Subendocardial anterolateral myocardial infarction.
   Primary hypothyroidism.

3. Enlarged pituitary fossa
   Sella has a double floor
   Erosion of the posterior clinoid process.

4. Bitemporal hemianopia.

5. Primary hypothyroidism.

6. Dynamic pituitary function testing to check for GH and ACTH reserve.

7. Non functioning pituitary adenoma and primary hypothyroidism.
   An alternative explanation is Primary hypothyroidism with secondary
   TSHoma causing hypopituitarism

8. Serum B12 level
   Gastric parietal antibodies
   Intrinsic factor antibodies

   Schilling test.

Answer 42

1. Aortic dissection
2. Transoesophageal echocardiography.
3. Marfan's syndrome

Answer 43

1. Anti GBM disease
   Microscopic polyarteritis nodosa.

   Wegener's granulomatosis

   Systemic lupus erythematosis

2. Renal biopsy

   Serum Anti GBM antibodies
   Serum ANCA
   Serum ANF

3. Haemodialysis.

   The presence of fluid overload, grossly elevated urea and a rising potassium are all indications for haemodialysis.

The combination of sever acute renal failure haemoptysis and alveolar shadowing on the chest X-ray are suggestive of a renal pulmonary syndrome. Any of the vasculitides in answer 1 above is capable of producing this clinical picture.

Answer 44

1. Primary biliary cirrhosis

2. IgM Anti-mitochondrial antibody titres
   Liver biopsy provided clotting is normal

Answer 45

1. Cranial diabetes insipidus

2. Head Injury, Pituitary Tumour, Sarcoidosis, Tuberculosis, Encephalitis,
   Histiocytosis X

The diagnosis of cranial insipidus is indicated by normalisation of the urine
osmolality following the administration of DDAVP (desmopressin), an ADH
analogue. Nephrogenic diabetes insipidus will not respond to DDAVP. It is due
to resistance of the distal renal tubular to the effects of ADH rather than a
deficiency of ADH. Several situations may cause nephrogenic diabetes insipidus
(see table).

> **Causes of Nephrogenic Diabetes Insipidus**
>
> Familial
> Fanconi's syndrome
> Hypokalaemia
> Hypercalcaemia
> Lithium Therapy
> Aminoglycosides
> Amphotericin

1. X-linked recessive.

2. 50%. His grandfather is affected, therefore his mother must be a carrier (affected males will transmit the abnormal gene to all female offspring). A female carrier will transmit the gene to 50% of all male offspring and 50% of all female offspring.

3. Nil. In relation to X-linked conditions males cannot be carriers as they have only one X-chromosone.

4. 25%. Her grandmother is a definite carrier.

5. Nil. There is no male to male transmission in X-linked conditions.

Answer 47

1. None

2. 50%. This is a pedigree of a condition inherited as an X-linked dominant trait. An affected male will not transmit the gene to any of his sons as they inherit his Y-chromosone. All his daughters inherit his X-chromosone (with genetic defect) and will be affected. An affected female will have 50% affected sons and 50% affected daughters.

Answer 48

1. Creutzfeld - Jakob Disease

   Differential diagnoses: Acute form of Alzheimers Disease, Cerebral metastases, Glioma or multifocal leucoencephalopathy

2. Brain Biopsy with immunostaining

1. Left bronchial carcinoma with metastases
   Metastatic bronchial carcinoma

2. Severe reduction in expiratory flow suggesting obstructive
   airways disease

   Reduced inspiratory flow suggesting extrathoracic airways obstruction

3. Infection
   Electrolyte imbalance
   Hypercalcaemia
   Cerebral metastases
   Encephalopathy (non-metastatic extrapulmonary manifestation)
   Hyponatraemia
   SIADH

4. Hypercalcaemia

5. **a.** Local and distant metastases
   b. Poor respiratory reserve

6. **Any of the following:**
   Oxygen
   Antibiotics
   IV fluids (Rehydration)
   Correct electrolyte disturbance or serum calcium
   Drain effusion
   Analgesia

Answer 50

A. Acute lymphoblastic leukaemia

✔ B. Acute myeloblastic leukaemia

C. Chronic lymphatic leukaemia

D. Chronic myeloid leukaemia

E. Infectious monucleosis

Myeloblasts are huge round cells. Some contain an inclusion in the cytoplasm which is termed an Auer rod.